**BAPTIST CONFESSION OF FAITH, 1689
AND
BAPTIST CATECHISM, 1693**

A WARFIELD INSTITUTE REPRINT

Published and Distributed by
THE WARFIELD INSTITUTE
warfieldinstitute@gmail.com

© 2019 by Matthew Smith
ISBN: 9781699821428

First Printing: October 2019

BAPTIST CONFESSION OF FAITH, 1689
AND
BAPTIST CATECHISM, 1693

Edited by Matthew Smith

Contents:

A. About The Warfield Institute

During the late Nineteenth and early Twentieth centuries, B.B. Warfield continued a line of men dedicated to the endeavor of Christian instruction. There are several convictions which undergird this endeavor. One conviction is that the Scriptures are θεόπνευστος – the God-breathed message which is supreme over any merely human authority. Another conviction is that truth is a prerequisite to holiness – from which, two corollaries easily follow. The first conclusion is that teaching truth is a reliable means of promoting holiness. The second conclusion is that there is something deeply flawed morally in those who neglect, minimize, and disregard truth.

On the foundation of these convictions and conclusions, the Warfield Institute seeks to continue the work of Christian instruction, and support faithful churches, by promoting a simple plan of Christian instruction consisting of three elements: (1) exegesis, (2) Scripture memorization, and (3) systematic theology.

Leaders at all levels will perform exegesis of Scripture as the primary means of teaching, and are required to model correct handling of the text so that all individuals will gain increasing maturity and competence in exegesis – especially subordinate leaders and future leaders.

Leaders will incorporate various forms of Scripture memorization into all contexts of Christian fellowship. Large public gatherings will feature regular reading of Scripture passages with the aim of increasing familiarization of those gathered with the text. Smaller gatherings, groups, and meetings will feature explicit opportunities for memorization at a priority not less than prayer or singing. A significant factor in selection of worship songs will be whether the content supports familiarization with Scripture. The regular use of a wide range of complete Psalms as worship songs will be adopted.

Leaders will regard systematic theology as the third essential element of Christian instruction. The presentation of truth disconnected from itself is inherently defective. To remedy this defect, the various elements of Scripture must be presented in a manner that displays their internal relations, that shows their harmony and consistency, and that vindicates their cogency against objections. This is the historic practice of catechizing.

For churches which already implement these elements, the Warfield Institute extends support and seeks to assist these efforts through the publications and programs which are made available. For churches which neglect, minimize, and disregard Scripture, the Warfield Institute wishes to state plainly that such action is sin, and requires appropriate repentance. A return to a focus on exegesis is long overdue. Replacement of current programs with a simple plan of exegesis, memorization, and catechizing will be a thoroughly justified reform.

B. About The Documents

Historically, the Protestant churches have utilized written confessions as a means of clarifying and systematizing Christian belief, and as a means of exposing and opposing error. It is recognized that without a systematic expression of the various elements of Scripture – an expression that displays their internal relations, that shows their harmony and consistency, and that vindicates their cogency against objections - individuals will either lack Christian instruction, or what instruction they receive will vary according to the individual knowledge, abilities, and dedication of their teachers. In order to prevent ignorance of God's word, confessions can supplement Scripture memorization and catechism-based instruction.

The Baptist believers of the English Separatist movement held convictions which were incompatible with the established churches of the 1600s. The central differences were belief that baptism should be performed only upon profession of faith, and congregational independence. These convictions are expressed in the Baptist Confession of Faith of 1689. From this confession, Benjamin Keach and William Collins developed a Baptist Catechism which was published in 1693.

Matthew Smith

14 October, 2019

C. About This Edition

At the beginning of the preface to *The Way of Life,* Charles Hodge summarized the Christian commitment to truth and the indispensable necessity of applying truth to the heart and mind in order to promote holiness. "It is one of the clearest principles of divine revelation, that holiness is the fruit of truth; and it is one of the plainest inferences from that principle, that the exhibition of the truth is the best means of promoting holiness."

It is the editor's conviction that lack of holiness in current congregations is directly related to lack of truth in the minds of the people in those congregations. In the current situation, individuals will receive Christian instruction only if their teachers diligently promote memorization of Scripture and provide other instruction which can be retained and applied. It should not be thought that longer, more complex teaching will necessarily constitute more profitable instruction. Rather, concise truth, known well enough to be retained decades later will change lives, while a constant stream of classes and multi-media will fail to be impactful. What is learned in one hour may be forgotten within six days; however, what is memorized may be impactful for six decades.

While in most endeavors results are never guaranteed, the diligent study of Scriptural truth is certain to be profitable. In conjunction with memorization of Scripture, diligent instruction in a sound confession and catechism will promote holiness. It is the editor's hope that an affordable edition of these documents will facilitate these goals.

Editions of these documents are available which include the reference citations for supporting Scripture (ISBN 9781699821022) and which omit these references (this edition). The edition with references is intended for detailed study and examination, and for defense of the material taught in the catechisms. The edition without references is intended for ease of use, for quick reference, and for memorization. Whichever edition is used, it should be understood that the documents are not intended to be understood apart from the cited Scripture, nor are they to be accepted on their own authority, but only as far as they accurately express the truths presented in Scripture.

Matthew Smith

14 October, 2019

1. Baptist Confession of Faith

Contents:

Chapter I. Of the Holy Scriptures.

1. The Holy Scripture is the only sufficient, certain, and infallible rule of all saving knowledge, faith, and obedience, although the light of nature, and the works of creation and providence do so far manifest the goodness, wisdom, and power of God, as to leave men inexcusable; yet are they not sufficient to give that knowledge of God and his will which is necessary unto salvation. Therefore it pleased the Lord at sundry times and in divers manners to reveal himself, and to declare that his will unto his church; and afterward for the better preserving and propagating of the truth, and for the more sure establishment and comfort of the church against the corruption of the flesh, and the malice of Satan, and of the world, to commit the same wholly unto writing; which maketh the Holy Scriptures to be most necessary, those former ways of God's revealing his will unto his people being now ceased.

2. Under the name of Holy Scripture, or the Word of God written, are now contained all the books of the Old and New Testaments, which are these:

OF THE OLD TESTAMENT: Genesis, Exodus, Leviticus, Numbers, Deuteronomy, Joshua, Judges, Ruth, I Samuel, II Samuel, I Kings, II Kings, I Chronicles, II Chronicles, Ezra, Nehemiah, Esther, Job, Psalms, Proverbs, Ecclesiastes, The Song of Solomon, Isaiah, Jeremiah, Lamentations, Ezekiel, Daniel, Hosea, Joel, Amos, Obadiah, Jonah, Micah, Nahum, Habakkuk, Zephaniah, Haggai, Zechariah, Malachi

OF THE NEW TESTAMENT: Matthew, Mark, Luke, John, The Acts of the Apostles, Paul's Epistle to the Romans, I Corinthians, II Corinthians, Galatians, Ephesians, Philippians, Colossians, I Thessalonians, II Thessalonians, I Timothy, II Timothy, To Titus, To Philemon, The Epistle to the Hebrews, Epistle of James, The first and second Epistles of Peter, The first, second, and third Epistles of John, The Epistle of Jude, The Revelation

All of which are given by the inspiration of God, to be the rule of faith and life.

3. The books commonly called Apocrypha, not being of divine inspiration, are no part of the canon or rule of the Scripture, and, therefore, are of no authority to the church of God, nor to be any otherwise approved or made use of than other human writings.

4. The authority of the Holy Scripture, for which it ought to be believed, dependeth not upon the testimony of any man or church, but wholly upon God (who is truth itself), the author thereof; therefore it is to be received because it is the Word of God.

5. We may be moved and induced by the testimony of the church of God to an high and reverent esteem of the Holy Scriptures; and the heavenliness of the matter, the efficacy of the doctrine, and the majesty of the style, the consent of all the parts, the scope of the whole (which is to give all glory to God), the full discovery it makes of the only way of man's salvation, and many other incomparable excellencies, and entire perfections thereof, are arguments whereby it doth abundantly evidence itself to be the Word of God; yet notwithstanding, our full persuasion and assurance of the infallible truth, and divine authority thereof, is from the inward work of the Holy Spirit bearing witness by and with the Word in our hearts.

6. The whole counsel of God concerning all things necessary for his own glory, man's salvation, faith and life, is either expressly set down or necessarily contained in the Holy Scripture: unto which nothing at any time is to be added, whether by new revelation of the Spirit, or traditions of men. Nevertheless, we acknowledge the inward illumination of the Spirit of God to be necessary for the saving understanding of such things as are revealed in the Word, and that there are some circumstances concerning the worship of God, and government of the church, common to human actions and societies, which are to be ordered by the light of nature and Christian prudence, according to the general rules of the Word, which are always to be observed.

7. All things in Scripture are not alike plain in themselves, nor alike clear unto all; yet those things which are necessary to be known, believed and observed for salvation, are so clearly propounded and opened in some place of Scripture or other, that not only the learned, but the unlearned, in a due use of ordinary means, may attain to a sufficient understanding of them.

8. The Old Testament in Hebrew (which was the native language of the people of God of old), and the New Testament in Greek (which at the time of the writing of it was most generally known to the nations), being immediately inspired by God, and by his singular care and providence kept pure in all ages, are therefore authentic; so as in all controversies of religion, the church is finally to appeal to them. But because these original tongues are not known to all the people of God, who have a right unto, and interest in the Scriptures, and are commanded in the fear of God to read and search them, therefore they are to be translated into the vulgar language of every nation unto which they come, that the Word of God dwelling plentifully in all, they may worship him in an acceptable manner, and through patience and comfort of the Scriptures may have hope.

9. The infallible rule of interpretation of Scripture is the Scripture itself; and therefore when there is a question about the true and full sense of any Scripture (which is not manifold, but one), it must be searched by other places that speak more clearly.

10. The supreme judge, by which all controversies of religion are to be determined, and all decrees of councils, opinions of ancient writers, doctrines of men, and private spirits, are to be examined, and in whose sentence we are to rest, can be no other but the Holy Scripture delivered by the Spirit, into which Scripture so delivered, our faith is finally resolved.

Chapter II. Of God and of the Holy Trinity.

1. The Lord our God is but one only living and true God; whose subsistence is in and of himself, infinite in being and perfection; whose essence cannot be comprehended by any but himself; a most pure spirit, invisible, without body, parts, or passions, who only hath immortality, dwelling in the light which no man can approach unto; who is immutable, immense, eternal, incomprehensible, almighty, every way infinite, most holy, most wise, most free, most absolute; working all things according to the counsel of his own immutable and most righteous will for his own glory; most loving, gracious, merciful, long-suffering, abundant in goodness and truth, forgiving iniquity, transgression, and sin; the rewarder of them that diligently seek him, and withal most just and terrible in his judgments, hating all sin, and who will by no means clear the guilty.

2. God, having all life, glory, goodness, blessedness, in and of himself, is alone in and unto himself all-sufficient, not standing in need of any creature which he hath made, nor deriving any glory from them, but only manifesting his own glory in, by, unto, and upon them; he is the alone fountain of all being, of whom, through whom, and to whom are all things, and he hath most sovereign dominion over all creatures, to do by them, for them, or upon them, whatsoever himself pleaseth; in his sight all things are open and manifest, his knowledge is infinite, infallible, and independent upon the creature, so as nothing is to him contingent or uncertain; he is most holy in all his counsels, in all his works, and in all his commands; to him is due from angels and men, whatsoever worship, service, or obedience, as creatures they owe unto the Creator, and whatever he is further pleased to require of them.

3. In this divine and infinite Being there are three subsistences, the Father, the Word or Son, and Holy Spirit, of one substance, power, and eternity, each having the whole divine essence, yet the essence undivided: the Father is of none, neither begotten nor proceeding; the Son is eternally begotten of the Father; the Holy Spirit proceeding from the Father and the Son; all infinite, without beginning, therefore but one God, who is not to be divided in nature and being, but distinguished by several peculiar relative properties and personal relations; which doctrine of the Trinity is the foundation of all our communion with God, and comfortable dependence on him.

Chapter III. Of God's Decree.

1. God hath decreed in himself, from all eternity, by the most wise and holy counsel of his own will, freely and unchangeably, all things, whatsoever comes to pass; yet so as thereby is God neither the author of sin nor hath fellowship with any therein; nor is violence offered to the will of the creature, nor yet is the liberty or contingency of second causes taken away, but rather established; in which appears his wisdom in disposing all things, and power and faithfulness in accomplishing his decree.

2. Although God knoweth whatsoever may or can come to pass, upon all supposed conditions, yet hath he not decreed anything, because he foresaw it as future, or as that which would come to pass upon such conditions.

3. By the decree of God, for the manifestation of his glory, some men and angels are predestinated, or foreordained to eternal life through Jesus Christ, to the praise of his glorious grace; others being left to act in their sin to their just condemnation, to the praise of his glorious justice.

4. These angels and men thus predestinated and foreordained, are particularly and unchangeably designed, and their number so certain and definite, that it cannot be either increased or diminished.

5. Those of mankind that are predestinated to life, God, before the foundation of the world was laid, according to his eternal and immutable purpose, and the secret counsel and good pleasure of his will, hath chosen in Christ unto everlasting glory, out of his mere free grace and love, without any other thing in the creature as a condition or cause moving him thereunto.

6. As God hath appointed the elect unto glory, so he hath, by the eternal and most free purpose of his will, foreordained all the means thereunto; wherefore they who are elected, being fallen in Adam, are redeemed by Christ, are effectually called unto faith in Christ, by his Spirit working in due season, are justified, adopted, sanctified, and kept by his power through faith unto salvation; neither are any other redeemed by Christ, or effectually called, justified, adopted, sanctified, and saved, but the elect only.

7. The doctrine of the high mystery of predestination is to be handled with special prudence and care, that men attending the will of God revealed in his Word, and yielding obedience thereunto, may, from the certainty of their effectual vocation, be assured of their eternal election; so shall this doctrine afford matter of praise, reverence, and admiration of God, and of humility, diligence, and abundant consolation to all that sincerely obey the gospel.

Chapter IV. Of Creation.

1. In the beginning it pleased God the Father, Son, and Holy Spirit, for the manifestation of the glory of his eternal power, wisdom, and goodness, to create or make the world, and all things therein, whether visible or invisible, in the space of six days, and all very good.

2. After God had made all other creatures, he created man, male and female, with reasonable and immortal souls, rendering them fit unto that life to God for which they were created; being made after the image of God, in knowledge, righteousness, and true holiness; having the law of God written in their hearts, and power to fulfill it, and yet under a possibility of transgressing, being left to the liberty of their own will, which was subject to change.

3. Besides the law written in their hearts, they received a command not to eat of the tree of knowledge of good and evil, which whilst they kept, they were happy in their communion with God, and had dominion over the creatures.

Chapter V. Of Divine Providence.

1. God the good Creator of all things, in his infinite power and wisdom doth uphold, direct, dispose, and govern all creatures and things, from the greatest even to the least, by his most wise and holy providence, to the end for the which they were created, according unto his infallible foreknowledge, and the free and immutable counsel of his own will; to the praise of the glory of his wisdom, power, justice, infinite goodness, and mercy.

2. Although in relation to the foreknowledge and decree of God, the first cause, all things come to pass immutably and infallibly; so that there is not anything befalls any by chance, or without his providence; yet by the same providence he ordereth them to fall out according to the nature of second causes, either necessarily, freely, or contingently.

3. God, in his ordinary providence maketh use of means, yet is free to work without, above, and against them at his pleasure.

4. The almighty power, unsearchable wisdom, and infinite goodness of God, so far manifest themselves in his providence, that his determinate counsel extendeth itself even to the first fall, and all other sinful actions both of angels and men; and that not by a bare permission, which also he most wisely and powerfully boundeth, and otherwise ordereth and governeth, in a manifold dispensation to his most holy ends; yet so, as the sinfulness of their acts proceedeth only from the creatures, and not from God, who, being most holy and righteous, neither is nor can be the author or approver of sin.

5. The most wise, righteous, and gracious God doth oftentimes leave for a season his own children to manifold temptations and the corruptions of their own hearts, to chastise them for their former sins, or to discover unto them the hidden strength of corruption and deceitfulness of their hearts, that they may be humbled; and to raise them to a more close and constant dependence for their support upon himself; and to make them more watchful against all future occasions of sin, and for other just and holy ends. So that whatsoever befalls any of his elect is by his appointment, for his glory, and their good.

6. As for those wicked and ungodly men whom God, as the righteous judge, for former sin doth blind and harden; from them he not only withholdeth his grace, whereby they might have been enlightened in their understanding, and wrought upon their hearts; but sometimes also withdraweth the gifts which they had, and exposeth them to such objects as their corruption makes occasion of sin; and withal, gives them over to their own lusts, the temptations of the world, and the power of Satan, whereby it comes to pass that they harden themselves, under those means which God useth for the softening of others.

7. As the providence of God doth in general reach to all creatures, so after a more special manner it taketh care of his church, and disposeth of all things to the good thereof.

Chapter VI. Of the Fall of Man, Of Sin, And of the Punishment Thereof.

1. Although God created man upright and perfect, and gave him a righteous law, which had been unto life had he kept it, and threatened death upon the breach thereof, yet he did not long abide in this honor; Satan using the subtlety of the serpent to subdue Eve, then by her seducing Adam, who, without any compulsion, did willfully transgress the law of their creation, and the command given unto them, in eating the forbidden fruit, which God was pleased, according to his wise and holy counsel to permit, having purposed to order it to his own glory.

2. Our first parents, by this sin, fell from their original righteousness and communion with God, and we in them whereby death came upon all: all becoming dead in sin, and wholly defiled in all the faculties and parts of soul and body.

3. They being the root, and by God's appointment, standing in the room and stead of all mankind, the guilt of the sin was imputed, and corrupted nature conveyed, to all their posterity descending from them by ordinary generation, being now conceived in sin, and by nature children of wrath, the servants of sin, the subjects of death, and all other miseries, spiritual, temporal, and eternal, unless the Lord Jesus set them free.

4. From this original corruption, whereby we are utterly indisposed, disabled, and made opposite to all good, and wholly inclined to all evil, do proceed all actual transgressions.

5. The corruption of nature, during this life, doth remain in those that are regenerated; and although it be through Christ pardoned and mortified, yet both itself, and the first motions thereof, are truly and properly sin.

8

Chapter VII. Of God's Covenant.

1. The distance between God and the creature is so great, that although reasonable creatures do owe obedience to him as their creator, yet they could never have attained the reward of life but by some voluntary condescension on God's part, which he hath been pleased to express by way of covenant.

2. Moreover, man having brought himself under the curse of the law by his fall, it pleased the Lord to make a covenant of grace, wherein he freely offereth unto sinners life and salvation by Jesus Christ, requiring of them faith in him, that they may be saved; and promising to give unto all those that are ordained unto eternal life, his Holy Spirit, to make them willing and able to believe.

3. This covenant is revealed in the gospel; first of all to Adam in the promise of salvation by the seed of the woman, and afterwards by farther steps, until the full discovery thereof was completed in the New Testament; and it is founded in that eternal covenant transaction that was between the Father and the Son about the redemption of the elect; and it is alone by the grace of this covenant that all the posterity of fallen Adam that ever were saved did obtain life and blessed immortality, man being now utterly incapable of acceptance with God upon those terms on which Adam stood in his state of innocency.

Chapter VIII. Of Christ the Mediator.

1. It pleased God, in His eternal purpose, to choose and ordain the Lord Jesus, his only begotten Son, according to the covenant made between them both, to be the mediator between God and man; the prophet, priest, and king; head and savior of the church, the heir of all things, and judge of the world; unto whom he did from all eternity give a people to be his seed and to be by him in time redeemed, called, justified, sanctified, and glorified.

2. The Son of God, the second person in the Holy Trinity, being very and eternal God, the brightness of the Father's glory, of one substance and equal with him who made the world, who upholdeth and governeth all things he hath made, did, when the fullness of time was come, take upon him man's nature, with all the essential properties and common infirmities thereof, yet without sin; being conceived by the Holy Spirit in the womb of the Virgin Mary, the Holy Spirit coming down upon her: and the power of the Most High overshadowing her; and so was made of a woman of the tribe of Judah, of the seed of Abraham and David according to the Scriptures; so that two whole, perfect, and distinct natures were inseparably joined together in one person, without conversion, composition, or confusion; which person is very God and very man, yet one Christ, the only mediator between God and man.

3. The Lord Jesus, in his human nature thus united to the divine, in the person of the Son, was sanctified and anointed with the Holy Spirit above measure, having in Him all the treasures of wisdom and knowledge; in whom it pleased the Father that all fullness should dwell, to the end that being holy, harmless, undefiled, and full of grace and truth, he might be thoroughly furnished to execute the office of mediator and surety; which office he took not upon himself, but was thereunto called by his Father; who also put all power and judgment in his hand, and gave him commandment to execute the same.

4. This office the Lord Jesus did most willingly undertake, which that he might discharge he was made under the law, and did perfectly fulfill it, and underwent the punishment due to us, which we should have borne and suffered, being made sin and a curse for us; enduring most grievous sorrows in his soul, and most painful sufferings in his body; was crucified, and died, and remained in the state of the dead, yet saw no corruption: on the third day he arose from the dead with the same body in which he suffered, with which he also ascended into heaven, and there sitteth at the right hand of his Father making intercession, and shall return to judge men and angels at the end of the world.

5. The Lord Jesus, by his perfect obedience and sacrifice of himself, which he through the eternal Spirit once offered up unto God, hath fully satisfied the justice of God, procured reconciliation, and purchased an everlasting inheritance in the kingdom of heaven, for all those whom the Father hath given unto Him.

6. Although the price of redemption was not actually paid by Christ till after his incarnation, yet the virtue, efficacy, and benefit thereof were communicated to the elect in all ages, successively from the beginning of the world, in and by those promises, types, and sacrifices wherein he was revealed, and signified to be the seed which should bruise the serpent's head; and the Lamb slain from the foundation of the world, being the same yesterday, and to-day and for ever.

7. Christ, in the work of mediation, acteth according to both natures, by each nature doing that which is proper to itself; yet by reason of the unity of the person, that which is proper to one nature is sometimes in Scripture, attributed to the person denominated by the other nature.

8. To all those for whom Christ hath obtained eternal redemption, he doth certainly and effectually apply and communicate the same, making intercession for them; uniting them to himself by his Spirit, revealing unto them, in and by his Word, the mystery of salvation, persuading them to believe and obey, governing their hearts by his Word and Spirit, and overcoming all their enemies by his almighty power and wisdom, in such manner and ways as are most consonant to his wonderful and unsearchable dispensation; and all of free and absolute grace, without any condition foreseen in them to procure it.

9. This office of mediator between God and man is proper only to Christ, who is the prophet, priest, and king of the church of God; and may not be either in whole, or any part thereof, transferred from him to any other.

10. This number and order of offices is necessary; for in respect of our ignorance, we stand in need of his prophetical office; and in respect of our alienation from God, and imperfection of the best of our services, we need his priestly office to reconcile us and present us acceptable unto God; and in respect to our averseness and utter inability to return to God, and for our rescue and security from our spiritual adversaries, we need his kingly office to convince, subdue, draw, uphold, deliver, and preserve us to his heavenly kingdom.

Chapter IX. Of Free Will.

1. God hath endued the will of man with that natural liberty and power of acting upon choice, that it is neither forced, nor by any necessity of nature determined to do good or evil.

2. Man, in his state of innocency, had freedom and power to will and to do that which was good and well-pleasing to God, but yet was unstable, so that he might fall from it.

3. Man, by his fall into a state of sin, hath wholly lost all ability of will to any spiritual good accompanying salvation; so as a natural man, being altogether averse from that good, and dead in sin, is not able by his own strength to convert himself, or to prepare himself thereunto.

4. When God converts a sinner, and translates him into the state of grace, he freeth him from his natural bondage under sin, and by his grace alone enables him freely to will and to do that which is spiritually good; yet so as that by reason of his remaining corruptions, he doth not perfectly, nor only will, that which is good, but doth also will that which is evil.

5. This will of man is made perfectly and immutably free to good alone in the state of glory only.

Chapter X. Of Effectual Calling.

1. Those whom God hath predestinated unto life, he is pleased in his appointed, and accepted time, effectually to call, by his Word and Spirit, out of that state of sin and death in which they are by nature, to grace and salvation by Jesus Christ; enlightening their minds spiritually and savingly to understand the things of God; taking away their heart of stone, and giving unto them a heart of flesh; renewing their wills, and by his almighty power determining them to that which is good, and effectually drawing them to Jesus Christ; yet so as they come most freely, being made willing by his grace.

2. This effectual call is of God's free and special grace alone, not from anything at all foreseen in man, nor from any power or agency in the creature, being wholly passive therein, being dead in sins and trespasses, until being quickened and renewed by the Holy Spirit; he is thereby enabled to answer this call, and to embrace the grace offered and conveyed in it, and that by no less power than that which raised up Christ from the dead.

3. Elect infants dying in infancy are regenerated and saved by Christ through the Spirit; who worketh when, and where, and how he pleases; so also are all elect persons, who are incapable of being outwardly called by the ministry of the Word.

4. Others not elected, although they may be called by the ministry of the Word, and may have some common operations of the Spirit, yet not being effectually drawn by the Father, they neither will nor can truly come to Christ, and therefore cannot be saved: much less can men that receive not the Christian religion be saved; be they never so diligent to frame their lives according to the light of nature and the law of that religion they do profess.

Chapter XI. Of Justification.

1. Those whom God effectually calleth, he also freely justifieth, not by infusing righteousness into them, but by pardoning their sins, and by accounting and accepting their persons as righteous; not for anything wrought in them, or done by them, but for Christ's sake alone; not by imputing faith itself, the act of believing, or any other evangelical obedience to them, as their righteousness; but by imputing Christ's active obedience unto the whole law, and passive obedience in his death for their whole and sole righteousness by faith, which faith they have not of themselves; it is the gift of God.

2. Faith thus receiving and resting on Christ and his righteousness, is the alone instrument of justification; yet it is not alone in the person justified, but is ever accompanied with all other saving graces, and is no dead faith, but worketh by love.

3. Christ, by his obedience and death, did fully discharge the debt of all those that are justified; and did, by the sacrifice of himself in the blood of his cross, undergoing in their stead the penalty due unto them, make a proper, real, and full satisfaction to God's justice in their behalf; yet, inasmuch as he was given by the Father for them, and his obedience and satisfaction accepted in their stead, and both freely, not for anything in them, their justification is only of free grace, that both the exact justice and rich grace of God might be glorified in the justification of sinners.

4. God did from all eternity decree to justify all the elect, and Christ did in the fullness of time die for their sins, and rise again for their justification; nevertheless, they are not justified personally, until the Holy Spirit doth in time due actually apply Christ unto them.

5. God doth continue to forgive the sins of those that are justified, and although they can never fall from the state of justification, yet they may, by their sins, fall under God's fatherly displeasure; and in that condition they have not usually the light of his countenance restored unto them, until they humble themselves, confess their sins, beg pardon, and renew their faith and repentance.

6. The justification of believers under the Old Testament was, in all these respects, one and the same with the justification of believers under the New Testament.

Chapter XII. Of Adoption.

All those that are justified, God vouchsafed, in and for the sake of his only Son Jesus Christ, to make partakers of the grace of adoption, by which they are taken into the number, and enjoy the liberties and privileges of the children of God, have his name put upon them, receive the spirit of adoption, have access to the throne of grace with boldness, are enabled to cry Abba, Father, are pitied, protected, provided for, and chastened by him as by a Father, yet never cast off, but sealed to the day of redemption, and inherit the promises as heirs of everlasting salvation.

Chapter XIII. Of Sanctification.

1. They who are united to Christ, effectually called, and regenerated, having a new heart and a new spirit created in them through the virtue of Christ's death and resurrection, are also farther sanctified, really and personally, through the same virtue, by His Word and Spirit dwelling in them; the dominion of the whole body of sin is destroyed, and the several lusts thereof are more and more weakened and mortified, and they more and more quickened and strengthened in all saving graces, to the practice of all true holiness, without which no man shall see the Lord.

2. This sanctification is throughout the whole man, yet imperfect in this life; there abideth still some remnants of corruption in every part, whence ariseth a continual and irreconcilable war; the flesh lusting against the Spirit, and the Spirit against the flesh.

3. In which war, although the remaining corruption for a time may much prevail, yet through the continual supply of strength from the sanctifying Spirit of Christ, the regenerate part doth overcome; and so the saints grow in grace, perfecting holiness in the fear of God, pressing after an heavenly life, in evangelical obedience to all the commands which Christ as Head and King, in His Word hath prescribed them.

Chapter XIV. Of Saving Faith.

1. The grace of faith, whereby the elect are enabled to believe to the saving of their souls, is the work of the Spirit of Christ in their hearts, and is ordinarily wrought by the ministry of the Word; by which also, and by the administration of baptism and the Lord's supper, prayer, and other means appointed of God, it is increased and strengthened.

2. By this faith a Christian believeth to be true whatsoever is revealed in the Word for the authority of God himself, and also apprehendeth an excellency therein above all other writings and all things in the world, as it bears forth the glory of God in his attributes, the excellency of Christ in his nature and offices, and the power and fullness of the Holy Spirit in his workings and operations: and so is enabled to cast his soul upon the truth thus believed; and also acteth differently upon that which each particular passage thereof containeth; yielding obedience to the commands, trembling at the threatenings, and embracing the promises of God for this life and that which is to come; but the principal acts of saving faith have immediate relation to Christ, accepting, receiving, and resting upon him alone for justification, sanctification, and eternal life, by virtue of the covenant of grace.

3. This faith, although it be different in degrees, and may be weak or strong, yet it is in the least degree of it different in the kind or nature of it, as is all other saving grace, from the faith and common grace of temporary believers; and therefore, though it may be many times assailed and weakened, yet it gets the victory, growing up in many to the attainment of a full assurance through Christ, who is both the author and finisher of our faith.

Chapter XV. Of Repentance Unto Life and Salvation.

1. Such of the elect as are converted at riper years, having sometime lived in the state of nature, and therein served divers lusts and pleasures, God in their effectual calling giveth them repentance unto life.

2. Whereas there is none that doth good and sinneth not, and the best of men may, through the power and deceitfulness of their corruption dwelling in them, with the prevalency of temptation, fall into great sins and provocations; God hath, in the covenant of grace, mercifully provided that believers so sinning and falling be renewed through repentance unto salvation.

3. This saving repentance is an evangelical grace, whereby a person, being by the Holy Spirit made sensible of the manifold evils of his sin, doth, by faith in Christ, humble himself for it with godly sorrow, detestation of it, and self-abhorrency, praying for pardon and strength of grace, with a purpose and endeavor, by supplies of the Spirit, to walk before God unto all well-pleasing in all things.

4. As repentance is to be continued through the whole course of our lives, upon the account of the body of death, and the motions thereof, so it is every man's duty to repent of his particular known sins particularly.

5. Such is the provision which God hath made through Christ in the covenant of grace for the preservation of believers unto salvation; that although there is no sin so small but it deserves damnation; yet there is no sin so great that it shall bring damnation on them that repent; which makes the constant preaching of repentance necessary.

Chapter XVI. Of Good Works.

1. Good works are only such as God hath commanded in his Holy Word, and not such as without the warrant thereof are devised by men out of blind zeal, or upon any pretense of good intentions.

2. These good works, done in obedience to God's commandments, are the fruits and evidences of a true and lively faith; and by them believers manifest their thankfulness, strengthen their assurance, edify their brethren, adorn the profession of the gospel, stop the mouths of the adversaries, and glorify God, whose workmanship they are, created in Christ Jesus thereunto, that having their fruit unto holiness they may have the end eternal life.

3. Their ability to do good works is not at all of themselves, but wholly from the Spirit of Christ; and that they may be enabled thereunto, besides the graces they have already received, there is necessary an actual influence of the same Holy Spirit, to work in them to will and to do of his good pleasure; yet they are not hereupon to grow negligent, as if they were not bound to perform any duty, unless upon a special motion of the Spirit, but they ought to be diligent in stirring up the grace of God that is in them.

4. They who in their obedience attain to the greatest height which is possible in this life, are so far from being able to supererogate, and to do more than God requires, as that they fall short of much which in duty they are bound to do.

5. We cannot by our best works merit pardon of sin or eternal life at the hand of God, by reason of the great disproportion that is between them and the glory to come, and the infinite distance that is between us and God, whom by them we can neither profit nor satisfy for the debt of our former sins; but when we have done all we can, we have done but our duty, and are unprofitable servants; and because as they are good they proceed from his Spirit, and as they are wrought by us they are defiled and mixed with so much weakness and imperfection, that they cannot endure the severity of God's punishment.

6. Yet notwithstanding the persons of believers being accepted through Christ, their good works also are accepted in him; not as though they were in this life wholly unblameable and unreprovable in God's sight, but that he, looking upon them in his Son, is pleased to accept and reward that which is sincere, although accompanied with many weaknesses and imperfections.

7. Works done by unregenerate men, although for the matter of them they may be things which God commands, and of good use both to themselves and others; yet because they proceed not from a heart purified by faith, nor are done in a right manner according to the word, nor to a right end, the glory of God, they are therefore sinful, and cannot please God, nor make a man meet to receive grace from God, and yet their neglect of them is more sinful and displeasing to God.

Chapter XVII. Of The Perseverance of the Saints.

1. Those whom God hath accepted in the beloved, effectually called and sanctified by his Spirit, and given the precious faith of his elect unto, can neither totally nor finally fall from the state of grace, but shall certainly persevere therein to the end, and be eternally saved, seeing the gifts and callings of God are without repentance, whence he still begets and nourisheth in them faith, repentance, love, joy, hope, and all the graces of the Spirit unto immortality; and though many storms and floods arise and beat against them, yet they shall never be able to take them off that foundation and rock which by faith they are fastened upon; notwithstanding, through unbelief and the temptations of Satan, the sensible sight of the light and love of God may for a time be clouded and obscured from them, yet he is still the same, and they shall be sure to be kept by the power of God unto salvation, where they shall enjoy their purchased possession, they being engraven upon the palm of his hands, and their names having been written in the book of life from all eternity.

2. This perseverance of the saints depends not upon their own free will, but upon the immutability of the decree of election, flowing from the free and unchangeable love of God the Father, upon the efficacy of the merit and intercession of Jesus Christ and union with him, the oath of God, the abiding of his Spirit, and the seed of God within them, and the nature of the covenant of grace; from all which ariseth also the certainty and infallibility thereof.

3. And though they may, through the temptation of Satan and of the world, the prevalency of corruption remaining in them, and the neglect of means of their preservation, fall into grievous sins, and for a time continue therein, whereby they incur God's displeasure and grieve his Holy Spirit, come to have their graces and comforts impaired, have their hearts hardened, and their consciences wounded, hurt and scandalize others, and bring temporal judgments upon themselves, yet shall they renew their repentance and be preserved through faith in Christ Jesus to the end.

Chapter XVIII. Of the Assurance of Grace and Salvation.

1. Although temporary believers, and other unregenerate men, may vainly deceive themselves with false hopes and carnal presumptions of being in the favor of God and state of salvation, which hope of theirs shall perish; yet such as truly believe in the Lord Jesus, and love him in sincerity, endeavoring to walk in all good conscience before him, may in this life be certainly assured that they are in the state of grace, and may rejoice in the hope of the glory of God, which hope shall never make them ashamed.

2. This certainty is not a bare conjectural and probable persuasion grounded upon a fallible hope, but an infallible assurance of faith founded on the blood and righteousness of Christ revealed in the Gospel; and also upon the inward evidence of those graces of the Spirit unto which promises are made, and on the testimony of the Spirit of adoption, witnessing with our spirits that we are the children of God; and, as a fruit thereof, keeping the heart both humble and holy.

3. This infallible assurance doth not so belong to the essence of faith, but that a true believer may wait long, and conflict with many difficulties before he be partaker of it; yet being enabled by the Spirit to know the things which are freely given him of God, he may, without extraordinary revelation, in the right use of means, attain thereunto: and therefore it is the duty of every one to give all diligence to make his calling and election sure, that thereby his heart may be enlarged in peace and joy in the Holy Spirit, in love and thankfulness to God, and in strength and cheerfulness in the duties of obedience, the proper fruits of this assurance; -so far is it from inclining men to looseness.

4. True believers may have the assurance of their salvation divers ways shaken, diminished, and intermitted; as by negligence in preserving of it, by falling into some special sin which woundeth the conscience and grieveth the Spirit; by some sudden or vehement temptation, by God's withdrawing the light of his countenance, and suffering even such as fear him to walk in darkness and to have no light, yet are they never destitute of the seed of God and life of faith, that love of Christ and the brethren, that sincerity of heart and conscience of duty out of which, by the operation of the Spirit, this assurance may in due time be revived, and by the which, in the meantime, they are preserved from utter despair.

Chapter XIX. Of the Law of God.

1. God gave to Adam a law of universal obedience written in his heart, and a particular precept of not eating the fruit of the tree of knowledge of good and evil; by which he bound him and all his posterity to personal, entire, exact, and perpetual obedience; promised life upon the fulfilling, and threatened death upon the breach of it, and endued him with power and ability to keep it.

2. The same law that was first written in the heart of man continued to be a perfect rule of righteousness after the fall, and was delivered by God upon Mount Sinai, in ten commandments, and written in two tables, the four first containing our duty towards God, and the other six, our duty to man.

3. Besides this law, commonly called moral, God was pleased to give to the people of Israel ceremonial laws, containing several typical ordinances, partly of worship, prefiguring Christ, his graces, actions, sufferings, and benefits; and partly holding forth divers instructions of moral duties, all which ceremonial laws being appointed only to the time of reformation, are, by Jesus Christ the true Messiah and only law-giver, who was furnished with power from the Father for that end abrogated and taken away.

4. To them also he gave sundry judicial laws, which expired together with the state of that people, not obliging any now by virtue of that institution; their general equity only being of moral use.

5. The moral law doth for ever bind all, as well justified persons as others, to the obedience thereof, and that not only in regard of the matter contained in it, but also in respect of the authority of God the Creator, who gave it; neither doth Christ in the Gospel any way dissolve, but much strengthen this obligation.

6. Although true believers be not under the law as a covenant of works, to be thereby justified or condemned, yet it is of great use to them as well as to others, in that as a rule of life, informing them of the will of God and their duty, it directs and binds them to walk accordingly; discovering also the sinful pollutions of their natures, hearts, and lives, so as examining themselves thereby, they may come to further conviction of, humiliation for, and hatred against, sin; together with a clearer sight of the need they have of Christ and the perfection of his obedience; it is likewise of use to the regenerate to restrain their corruptions, in that it forbids sin; and the threatenings of it serve to shew what even their sins deserve, and what afflictions in this life they may expect for them, although freed from the curse and unallayed rigor thereof. The promises of it likewise shew them God's approbation of obedience, and what blessings they may expect upon the performance thereof, though not as due to them by the law as a covenant of works; so as man's doing good and refraining from evil, because the law encourageth to the one and deterreth from the other, is no evidence of his being under the law and not under grace.

7. Neither are the aforementioned uses of the law contrary to the grace of the Gospel, but do sweetly comply with it, the Spirit of Christ subduing and enabling the will of man to do that freely and cheerfully which the will of God, revealed in the law, requireth to be done.

Chapter XX. Of the Gospel, and of the Extent of the Grace Thereof.

1. The covenant of works being broken by sin, and made unprofitable unto life, God was pleased to give forth the promise of Christ, the seed of the woman, as the means of calling the elect, and begetting in them faith and repentance; in this promise the gospel, as to the substance of it, was revealed, and [is] therein effectual for the conversion and salvation of sinners.

2. This promise of Christ, and salvation by him, is revealed only by the Word of God; neither do the works of creation or providence, with the light of nature, make discovery of Christ, or of grace by him, so much as in a general or obscure way; much less that men destitute of the revelation of Him by the promise or gospel, should be enabled thereby to attain saving faith or repentance.

3. The revelation of the gospel unto sinners, made in divers times and by sundry parts, with the addition of promises and precepts for the obedience required therein, as to the nations and persons to whom it is granted, is merely of the sovereign will and good pleasure of God; not being annexed by virtue of any promise to the due improvement of men's natural abilities, by virtue of common light received without it, which none ever did make, or can do so; and therefore in all ages, the preaching of the gospel has been granted unto persons and nations, as to the extent or straitening of it, in great variety, according to the counsel of the will of God.

4. Although the gospel be the only outward means of revealing Christ and saving grace, and is, as such, abundantly sufficient thereunto; yet that men who are dead in trespasses may be born again, quickened or regenerated, there is moreover necessary an effectual insuperable work of the Holy Spirit upon the whole soul, for the producing in them a new spiritual life; without which no other means will effect their conversion unto God.

Chapter XXI. Of Christian Liberty and Liberty of Conscience.

1. The liberty which Christ hath purchased for believers under the gospel, consists in their freedom from the guilt of sin, the condemning wrath of God, the rigor and curse of the law, and in their being delivered from this present evil world, bondage to Satan, and dominion of sin, from the evil of afflictions, the fear and sting of death, the victory of the grave, and ever- lasting damnation: as also in their free access to God, and their yielding obedience unto Him, not out of slavish fear, but a child-like love and willing mind.

All which were common also to believers under the law for the substance of them; but under the New Testament the liberty of Christians is further enlarged, in their freedom from the yoke of a ceremonial law, to which the Jewish church was subjected, and in greater boldness of access to the throne of grace, and in fuller communications of the free Spirit of God, than believers under the law did ordinarily partake of.

2. God alone is Lord of the conscience, and hath left it free from the doctrines and commandments of men which are in any thing contrary to his word, or not contained in it. So that to believe such doctrines, or obey such commands out of conscience, is to betray true liberty of conscience; and the requiring of an implicit faith, an absolute and blind obedience, is to destroy liberty of conscience and reason also.

3. They who upon pretense of Christian liberty do practice any sin, or cherish any sinful lust, as they do thereby pervert the main design of the grace of the gospel to their own destruction, so they wholly destroy the end of Christian liberty, which is, that being delivered out of the hands of all our enemies, we might serve the Lord without fear, in holiness and righteousness before Him, all the days of our lives.

Chapter 22: Of Religious Worship and the Sabbath Day

1. The light of nature shews that there is a God, who hath lordship and sovereignty over all; is just, good and doth good unto all; and is therefore to be feared, loved, praised, called upon, trusted in, and served, with all the heart and all the soul, and with all the might. But the acceptable way of worshiping the true God, is instituted by himself, and so limited by his own revealed will, that he may not be worshiped according to the imagination and devices of men, nor the suggestions of Satan, under any visible representations, or any other way not prescribed in the Holy Scriptures.

2. Religious worship is to be given to God the Father, Son, and Holy Spirit, and to him alone; not to angels, saints, or any other creatures; and since the fall, not without a mediator, nor in the mediation of any other but Christ alone.

3. Prayer, with thanksgiving, being one part of natural worship, is by God required of all men. But that it may be accepted, it is to be made in the name of the Son, by the help of the Spirit, according to his will; with understanding, reverence, humility, fervency, faith, love, and perseverance; and when with others, in a known tongue.

4. Prayer is to be made for things lawful, and for all sorts of men living, or that shall live hereafter; but not for the dead, nor for those of whom it may be known that they have sinned the sin unto death.

5. The reading of the Scriptures, preaching, and hearing the Word of God, teaching and admonishing one another in psalms, hymns, and spiritual songs, singing with grace in our hearts to the Lord; as also the administration of baptism, and the Lord's supper, are all parts of religious worship of God, to be performed in obedience to him, with understanding, faith, reverence, and godly fear; moreover, solemn humiliation, with fastings, and thanksgivings, upon special occasions, ought to be used in an holy and religious manner.

6. Neither prayer nor any other part of religious worship, is now under the gospel, tied unto, or made more acceptable by any place in which it is performed, or towards which it is directed; but God is to be worshiped everywhere in spirit and in truth; as in private families daily, and in secret each one by himself; so more solemnly in the public assemblies, which are not carelessly nor willfully to be neglected or forsaken, when God by his word or providence calleth thereunto.

7. As it is the law of nature, that in general a proportion of time, by God's appointment, be set apart for the worship of God, so by his Word, in a positive moral, and perpetual commandment, binding all men, in all ages, he hath particularly appointed one day in seven for a sabbath to be kept holy unto him, which from the beginning of the world to the resurrection of Christ was the last day of the week, and from the resurrection of Christ was changed into the first day of the week, which is called the Lord's day: and is to be continued to the end of the world as the Christian Sabbath, the observation of the last day of the week being abolished.

8. The sabbath is then kept holy unto the Lord, when men, after a due preparing of their hearts, and ordering their common affairs aforehand, do not only observe an holy rest all day, from their own works, words and thoughts, about their worldly employment and recreations, but are also taken up the whole time in the public and private exercises of his worship, and in the duties of necessity and mercy.

Chapter XXIII. Of Lawful Oaths and Vows.

1. A lawful oath is a part of religious worship, wherein the person swearing in truth, righteousness, and judgment, solemnly calleth God to witness what he sweareth, and to judge him according to the truth or falseness thereof.

2. The name of God only is that by which men ought to swear; and therein it is to be used, with all holy fear and reverence; therefore to swear vainly or rashly by that glorious and dreadful name, or to swear at all by any other thing, is sinful, and to be abhorred; yet as in matter of weight and moment, for confirmation of truth, and ending all strife, an oath is warranted by the word of God; so a lawful oath being imposed by lawful authority in such matters, ought to be taken.

3. Whosoever taketh an oath warranted by the Word of God, ought duly to consider the weightiness of so solemn an act, and therein to avouch nothing but what he knoweth to be truth; for that by rash, false, and vain oaths, the Lord is provoked, and for them this land mourns.

4. An oath is to be taken in the plain and common sense of the words, without equivocation or mental reservation.

5. A vow, which is not to be made to any creature, but to God alone, is to be made and performed with all religious care and faithfulness; but popish monastical vows of perpetual single life, professed poverty, and regular obedience, are so far from being degrees of higher perfection, that they are superstitious and sinful snares, in which no Christian may entangle himself.

Chapter XXIV. Of the Civil Magistrate.

1. God, the supreme Lord and King of all the world, hath ordained civil magistrates to be under him, over the people, for his own glory and the public good; and to this end hath armed them with the power of the sword, for defense and encouragement of them that do good, and for the punishment of evil doers.

2. It is lawful for Christians to accept and execute the office of a magistrate when called there unto; in the management whereof, as they ought especially to maintain justice and peace, according to the wholesome laws of each kingdom and commonwealth, so for that end they may lawfully now, under the New Testament wage war upon just and necessary occasions.

3. Civil magistrates being set up by God for the ends aforesaid; subjection, in all lawful things commanded by them, ought to be yielded by us in the Lord, not only for wrath, but for conscience sake; and we ought to make supplications and prayers for kings and all that are in authority, that under them we may live a quiet and peaceable life, in all godliness and honesty.

Chapter XXV. Of Marriage.

1. Marriage is to be between one man and one woman; neither is it lawful for any man to have more than one wife, nor for any woman to have more than one husband at the same time.

2. Marriage was ordained for the mutual help of husband and wife, for the increase of mankind with a legitimate issue, and the preventing of uncleanness.

3. It is the duty of Christians to marry in the Lord; and therefore such as profess the true religion, should not marry with infidels, or idolaters; neither should such as are godly, be unequally yoked, by marrying with such as are wicked in their life, or maintain damnable heresy.

4. Marriage ought not to be within the degrees of consanguinity or affinity, forbidden in the Word; nor can such incestuous marriages ever be made lawful, by any law of man or consent of parties, so as those persons may live together as man and wife.

Chapter XXVI. Of the Church.

1. The catholic or universal church, which (with respect to the internal work of the Spirit and truth of grace) may be called invisible, consists of the whole number of the elect, that have been, are, or shall be gathered into one, under Christ, the head thereof; and is the spouse, the body, the fullness of him that filleth all in all.

2. All persons throughout the world, professing the faith of the gospel, and obedience unto God by Christ according unto it, not destroying their own profession by any errors everting the foundation, or unholiness of conversation, are and may be called visible saints; and of such ought all particular congregations to be constituted.

3. The purest churches under heaven are subject to mixture and error; and some have so degenerated as to become no churches of Christ, but synagogues of Satan; nevertheless Christ always hath had, and ever shall have a kingdom in this world, to the end thereof, of such as believe in him, and make profession of his name.

4. The Lord Jesus Christ is the Head of the church, in whom, by the appointment of the Father, all power for the calling, institution, order or government of the church, is invested in a supreme and sovereign manner; neither can the Pope of Rome in any sense be head thereof, but is that antichrist, that man of sin, and son of perdition, that exalteth himself in the church against Christ, and all that is called God; whom the Lord shall destroy with the brightness of his coming.

5. In the execution of this power wherewith he is so intrusted, the Lord Jesus calleth out of the world unto himself, through the ministry of his word, by his Spirit, those that are given unto him by his Father, that they may walk before him in all the ways of obedience, which he prescribeth to them in his word. Those thus called, he commandeth to walk together in particular societies, or churches, for their mutual edification, and the due performance of that public worship, which he requireth of them in the world.

6. The members of these churches are saints by calling, visibly manifesting and evidencing (in and by their profession and walking) their obedience unto that call of Christ; and do willingly consent to walk together, according to the appointment of Christ; giving up themselves to the Lord, and one to another, by the will of God, in professed subjection to the ordinances of the Gospel.

7. To each of these churches thus gathered, according to his mind declared in his word, he hath given all that power and authority, which is in any way needful for their carrying on that order in worship and discipline, which he hath instituted for them to observe; with commands and rules for the due and right exerting, and executing of that power.

8. A particular church, gathered and completely organized according to the mind of Christ, consists of officers and members; and the officers appointed by Christ to be chosen and set apart by the church (so called and gathered), for the peculiar administration of ordinances, and execution of power or duty, which he intrusts them with, or calls them to, to be continued to the end of the world, are bishops or elders, and deacons.

9. The way appointed by Christ for the calling of any person, fitted and gifted by the Holy Spirit, unto the office of bishop or elder in a church, is, that he be chosen thereunto by the common suffrage of the church itself; and solemnly set apart by fasting and prayer, with imposition of hands of the eldership of the church, if there be any before constituted therein; and of a deacon that he be chosen by the like suffrage, and set apart by prayer, and the like imposition of hands.

10. The work of pastors being constantly to attend the service of Christ, in his churches, in the ministry of the word and prayer, with watching for their souls, as they that must give an account to Him; it is incumbent on the churches to whom they minister, not only to give them all due respect, but also to communicate to them of all their good things according to their ability, so as they may have a comfortable supply, without being themselves entangled in secular affairs; and may also be capable of exercising hospitality towards others; and this is required by the law of nature, and by the express order of our Lord Jesus, who hath ordained that they that preach the Gospel should live of the Gospel.

11. Although it be incumbent on the bishops or pastors of the churches, to be instant in preaching the word, by way of office, yet the work of preaching the word is not so peculiarly confined to them but that others also gifted and fitted by the Holy Spirit for it, and approved and called by the church, may and ought to perform it.

12. As all believers are bound to join themselves to particular churches, when and where they have opportunity so to do; so all that are admitted unto the privileges of a church, are also under the censures and government thereof, according to the rule of Christ.

13. No church members, upon any offense taken by them, having performed their duty required of them towards the person they are offended at, ought to disturb any church-order, or absent themselves from the assemblies of the church, or administration of any ordinances, upon the account of such offense at any of their fellow members, but to wait upon Christ, in the further proceeding of the church.

14. As each church, and all the members of it, are bound to pray continually for the good and prosperity of all the churches of Christ, in all places, and upon all occasions to further every one within the bounds of their places and callings, in the exercise of their gifts and graces, so the churches, when planted by the providence of God, so as they may enjoy opportunity and advantage for it, ought to hold communion among themselves, for their peace, increase of love, and mutual edification.

15. In cases of difficulties or differences, either in point of doctrine or administration, wherein either the churches in general are concerned, or any one church, in their peace, union, and edification; or any member or members of any church are injured, in or by any proceedings in censures not agreeable to truth and order: it is according to the mind of Christ, that many churches holding communion together, do, by their messengers, meet to consider, and give their advice in or about that matter in difference, to be reported to all the churches concerned; howbeit these messengers assembled, are not intrusted with any church-power properly so called; or with any jurisdiction over the churches themselves, to exercise any censures either over any churches or persons; or to impose their determination on the churches or officers.

Chapter XXVII. Of the Communion of Saints.

1. All saints that are united to Jesus Christ, their head, by his Spirit, and faith, although they are not made thereby one person with him, have fellowship in his graces, sufferings, death, resurrection, and glory; and, being united to one another in love, they have communion in each others gifts and graces, and are obliged to the performance of such duties, public and private, in an orderly way, as do conduce to their mutual good, both in the inward and outward man.

2. Saints by profession are bound to maintain an holy fellowship and communion in the worship of God, and in performing such other spiritual services as tend to their mutual edification; as also in relieving each other in outward things according to their several abilities, and necessities; which communion, according to the rule of the gospel, though especially to be exercised by them, in the relation wherein they stand, whether in families, or churches, yet, as God offereth opportunity, is to be extended to all the household of faith, even all those who in every place call upon the name of the Lord Jesus; nevertheless their communion one with another as saints, doth not take away or infringe the title or propriety which each man hath in his goods and possessions.

Chapter XXVIII. Of Baptism and the Lord's Supper.

1. Baptism and the Lord's Supper are ordinances of positive and sovereign institution, appointed by the Lord Jesus, the only lawgiver, to be continued in his church to the end of the world.

2. These holy appointments are to be administered by those only who are qualified and thereunto called, according to the commission of Christ.

Chapter XXIX. Of Baptism.

1. Baptism is an ordinance of the New Testament, ordained by Jesus Christ, to be unto the party baptized, a sign of his fellowship with him, in his death and resurrection; of his being engrafted into him; of remission of sins; and of giving up into God, through Jesus Christ, to live and walk in newness of life.

2. Those who do actually profess repentance towards God, faith in, and obedience to, our Lord Jesus Christ, are the only proper subjects of this ordinance.

3. The outward element to be used in this ordinance is water, wherein the party is to be baptized, in the name of the Father, and of the Son, and of the Holy Spirit.

4. Immersion, or dipping of the person in water, is necessary to the due administration of this ordinance.

Chapter XXX. Of the Lord's Supper.

1. The supper of the Lord Jesus was instituted by him the same night wherein he was betrayed, to be observed in his churches, unto the end of the world, for the perpetual remembrance, and shewing forth the sacrifice of himself in his death, confirmation of the faith of believers in all the benefits thereof, their spiritual nourishment, and growth in him, their further engagement in, and to all duties which they owe to him; and to be a bond and pledge of their communion with him, and with each other.

2. In this ordinance Christ is not offered up to his Father, nor any real sacrifice made at all for remission of sin of the quick or dead, but only a memorial of that one offering up of himself by himself upon the cross, once for all; and a spiritual oblation of all possible praise unto God for the same. So that the popish sacrifice of the mass, as they call it, is most abominable, injurious to Christ's own sacrifice the alone propitiation for all the sins of the elect.

3. The Lord Jesus hath, in this ordinance, appointed his ministers to pray, and bless the elements of bread and wine, and thereby to set them apart from a common to a holy use, and to take and break the bread; to take the cup, and, they communicating also themselves, to give both to the communicants.

4. The denial of the cup to the people, worshiping the elements, the lifting them up, or carrying them about for adoration, and reserving them for any pretended religious use, are all contrary to the nature of this ordinance, and to the institution of Christ.

5. The outward elements in this ordinance, duly set apart to the use ordained by Christ, have such relation to him crucified, as that truly, although in terms used figuratively, they are sometimes called by the names of the things they represent, to wit, the body and blood of Christ, albeit, in substance and nature, they still remain truly and only bread and wine, as they were before.

6. That doctrine which maintains a change of the substance of bread and wine, into the substance of Christ's body and blood, commonly called transubstantiation, by consecration of a priest, or by any other way, is repugnant not to Scripture alone, but even to common sense and reason, overthroweth the nature of the ordinance, and hath been, and is, the cause of manifold superstitions, yea, of gross idolatries.

7. Worthy receivers, outwardly partaking of the visible elements in this ordinance, do then also inwardly by faith, really and indeed, yet not carnally and corporally, but spiritually receive, and feed upon Christ crucified, and all the benefits of his death; the body and blood of Christ being then not corporally or carnally, but spiritually present to the faith of believers in that ordinance, as the elements themselves are to their outward senses.

8. All ignorant and ungodly persons, as they are unfit to enjoy communion with Christ, so are they unworthy of the Lord's table, and cannot, without great sin against him, while they remain such, partake of these holy mysteries, or be admitted thereunto; yea, whosoever shall receive unworthily, are guilty of the body and blood of the Lord, eating and drinking judgment to themselves.

Chapter XXXI. Of the State of Man after Death and Of the Resurrection of the Dead.

1. The bodies of men after death return to dust, and see corruption; but their souls, which neither die nor sleep, having an immortal subsistence, immediately return to God who gave them. The souls of the righteous being then made perfect in holiness, are received into paradise, where they are with Christ, and behold the face of God in light and glory, waiting for the full redemption of their bodies; and the souls of the wicked are cast into hell; where they remain in torment and utter darkness, reserved to the judgment of the great day; besides these two places, for souls separated from their bodies, the Scripture acknowledgeth none.

2. At the last day, such of the saints as are found alive, shall not sleep, but be changed; and all the dead shall be raised up with the selfsame bodies, and none other; although with different qualities, which shall be united again to their souls forever.

3. The bodies of the unjust shall, by the power of Christ, be raised to dishonor; the bodies of the just, by his Spirit, unto honor, and be made conformable to his own glorious body.

Chapter XXXII. Of the Last Judgment

1. God hath appointed a day wherein he will judge the world in righteousness, by Jesus Christ; to whom all power and judgment is given of the Father; in which day, not only the apostate angels shall be judged, but likewise all persons that have lived upon the earth shall appear before the tribunal of Christ, to give an account of their thoughts, words, and deeds, and to receive according to what they have done in the body, whether good or evil.

2. The end of God's appointing this day, is for the manifestation of the glory of his mercy, in the eternal salvation of the elect; and of his justice, in the eternal damnation of the reprobate, who are wicked and disobedient; for then shall the righteous go into everlasting life, and receive that fullness of joy and glory with everlasting rewards, in the presence of the Lord; but the wicked, who know not God, and obey not the gospel of Jesus Christ, shall be cast aside into everlasting torments, and punished with everlasting destruction, from the presence of the Lord, and from the glory of his power.

3. As Christ would have us to be certainly persuaded that there shall be a day of judgment, both to deter all men from sin, and for the greater consolation of the godly in their adversity, so will he have the day unknown to men, that they may shake off all carnal security, and be always watchful, because they know not at what hour the Lord will come, and may ever be prepared to say, Come Lord Jesus; come quickly. Amen.

Closing Statement & Signatories

We the MINISTERS, and MESSENGERS of, and concerned for upwards of, one hundred BAPTIZED CHURCHES, in England and Wales (denying Arminianisim), being met together in London, from the third of the seventh month to the eleventh of the same, 1689, to consider of some things that might be for the glory of God, and the good of these congregations, have thought meet (for the satisfaction of all other Christians that differ from us in the point of Baptism) to recommend to their perusal the confession of our faith, which confession we own, as containing the doctrine of our faith and practice, and do desire that the members of our churches respectively do furnish themselves therewith.

2. Baptist Catechism

1. Who is the first and best of beings?

God is the first and best of beings.

2. What is the chief end of man?

Man's chief end is to glorify God and to enjoy Him forever.

3. How do we know there is a God?

The light of nature in man, and the works of God, plainly declare that there is a God; but His Word and Spirit only, do effectually reveal Him unto us for our salvation.

4. What is the Word of God?

The Scriptures of the Old and New Testaments, being given by divine inspiration, are the Word of God, the only infallible rule of faith and practice.

5. How do we know that the Bible is the Word of God?

The Bible evidences itself to be God's Word by the heavenliness of its doctrine, the unity of its parts, its power to convert sinners and to edify saints; but the Spirit of God only, bearing witness by and with the Scriptures in our hearts, is able fully to persuade us that the Bible is the Word of God.

6. May all men make use of the Scriptures?

All men are not only permitted, but commanded and exhorted, to read, hear, and understand the Scriptures.

7. What do the Scriptures principally teach?

The Scriptures principally teach what man is to believe concerning God and what duty God requires of man.

8. What is God?

God is a Spirit, infinite, eternal, and unchangeable in His being, wisdom, power, holiness, justice, goodness and truth.

9. Are there more gods than one?

There is but one only, the living and true God.

10. How many persons are there in the Godhead?

There are three persons in the Godhead, the Father, the Son, and the Holy

Spirit; and these three are one God, the same in essence, equal in power and glory.

11. What are the decrees of God?

The decrees of God are His eternal purpose, according to the counsel of His will, whereby for His own glory, He has fore-ordained whatsoever comes to pass.

12. How does God execute His decrees?

God executes His decrees in the works of creation and providence.

13. What is the work of creation?

The work of creation is God's making all things of nothing, by the Word of His power, in the space of six days, and all very good.

14. How did God create man?

God created man male and female, after His own image, in knowledge, righteousness, and holiness, with dominion over the creatures.

15. What are God's works of providence?

God's works of providence are His most holy, wise, and powerful preserving and governing all His creatures, and all their actions.

16. What special act of providence did God exercise towards man, in the estate wherein he was created?

When God had created man, He entered into a covenant of works with him, upon condition of perfect obedience, forbidding him to eat of the tree of the knowledge of good and evil, upon pain of death.

17. Did our first parents continue in the estate wherein they were created?

Our first parents, being left to the freedom of their own will, fell from the estate wherein they were created, by sinning against God.

18. What is sin?

Sin is any want of conformity unto, or transgression of, the law of God.

19. What was the sin whereby our first parents fell from the estate wherein they were created?

The sin whereby our first parents fell from the estate wherein they were created, was their eating the forbidden fruit.

20. Did all mankind fall in Adam's first transgression?

The covenant being made with Adam, not only for himself but for his posterity, all mankind, descending from him by ordinary generation, sinned in him, and fell with him in his first transgression.

21. Into what estate did the fall bring mankind?

The fall brought mankind into an estate of sin and misery.

22. Wherein consists the sinfulness of that estate whereunto man fell?

The sinfulness of that estate whereunto man fell, consists in the guilt of Adam's first sin, the want of original righteousness, and the corruption of his whole nature, which is commonly called original sin, together with all actual transgressions which proceed from it.

23. What is the misery of that estate whereunto man fell?

All mankind, by their fall lost communion with God, are under His wrath and curse, and made liable to all the miseries of this life, to death itself, and to the pains of hell forever.

24. Did God leave all mankind to perish in the estate of sin and misery?

God, out of His mere good pleasure, from all eternity, having chosen a people to everlasting life, did enter into a covenant of grace, to deliver them out of the estate of sin and misery, and to bring them into an estate of salvation, by a Redeemer.

25. Who is the Redeemer of God's elect?

The only Redeemer of God's elect is the Lord Jesus Christ, who, being the eternal Son of God, became man, and so was and continues to be God and man, in two distinct natures and one person, forever.

26. How did Christ, being the Son of God, become man?

Christ, the Son of God became man by taking to himself a true body and a reasonable soul; being conceived by the power of the Holy Spirit in the womb of the Virgin Mary and born of her, yet without sin.

27. What offices does Christ execute as our Redeemer?

Christ, as our Redeemer, executes the offices of a prophet, of a priest, and of a king, both in His estate of humiliation and exaltation.

28. How does Christ execute the office of a prophet?

Christ executes the office of a prophet, in revealing to us, by this Word and Spirit, the will of God for our salvation.

29. How does Christ execute the office of a priest?

Christ executes the office of a priest, in His once offering up of Himself, a sacrifice to satisfy divine justice, and reconcile us to God, and in making continual intercession for us.

30. How does Christ execute the office of a king?

Christ executes the office of a king, in subduing us to Himself, in ruling and defending us, and in restraining and conquering all His and our enemies.

31. Wherein did Christ's humiliation consist?

Christ's humiliation consisted in His being born, and that in a low condition, made under the law, undergoing the miseries of this life, the wrath of God, and the cursed death of the cross, in being buried, and continuing under the power of death for a time.

32. Wherein consists Christ's exaltation?

Christ's exaltation consists in His rising again from the dead on the third day, in ascending up into heaven, in sitting at the right hand of God the Father, and in coming to judge the world at the last day.

33. How are we made partakers of the redemption purchased by Christ?

We are made partakers of the redemption purchased by Christ, by the effectual application of it to us, by His Holy Spirit.

34. How does the Spirit apply to us the redemption purchased by Christ?

The Spirit applies to us the redemption purchased by Christ, by working faith in us, and thereby uniting us to Christ in our effectual calling.

35. What is effectual calling?

Effectual calling is the work of God's Spirit, whereby, convincing us of our sin and misery, enlightening our minds in the knowledge of Christ, and renewing our wills, He does persuade and enable us to embrace Jesus Christ, freely offered to us in the Gospel.

36. What benefits do they that are effectually called, partake of in this life?

They that are effectually called, do in this life partake of justification, adoption, sanctification, and the several benefits which in this life do either accompany or flow from them.

37. What is justification?

Justification is an act of God's free grace, wherein He pardons all our sins, and accepts us as righteous in His sight, only for the righteousness of Christ imputed to us, and received by faith alone.

38. What is adoption?

Adoption is an act of God's free grace, whereby we are received into the number, and have a right to all the privileges of the sons of God.

39. What is sanctification?

Sanctification is a work of God's free grace whereby we are renewed in the whole man after the image of God, and are enabled more and more to die unto sin, and live unto righteousness.

40. What are the benefits which in this life do accompany or flow from justification, adoption, and sanctification?

The benefits which in this life do accompany or flow from justification, adoption, and sanctification, are, assurance of God's love, peace of conscience, joy in the Holy Spirit, increase of grace, and perseverance therein to the end.

41. What benefits do believers receive from Christ at death?

The souls of believers are at death made perfect in holiness, and do immediately pass into glory, and their bodies, being still united to Christ, do rest in their graves till the resurrection.

42. What benefits do believers receive from Christ at the Resurrection?

At the resurrection, believers become raised up in glory, shall be openly acknowledged and acquitted in the day of judgment, and made perfectly blessed in the full enjoyment of God to all eternity.

43. What shall be done to the wicked at death?

The souls of the wicked shall at death, be cast into the torments of hell, and their bodies lie in their graves till the resurrection and judgment of the great day.

44. What shall be done to the wicked at the day of judgment?

At the day of judgment, the bodies of the wicked, being raised out of their graves, shall be sentenced, together with their souls, to unspeakable torments with the devil and his angels forever.

45. What is the duty which God requires of man?

The duty which God requires of man, is obedience to His revealed will.

46. What did God at first reveal to man for the rule of his obedience?

The rule which God at first revealed to man for his obedience was the moral law.

47. Where is the moral law summarily comprehended?

The moral law is summarily comprehended in the Ten Commandments.

48. What is the sum of the Ten Commandments?

The sum of the Ten Commandments is, to love the Lord our God, with all our heart, with all our soul, with all our strength, and with all our mind; and our neighbor as ourselves.

49. What is the preface to the Ten Commandments?

The preface to the Ten Commandments is, "I am the Lord thy God, which have brought thee out of the land of Egypt, out of the house of bondage."

50. What does the preface to the Ten Commandments teach us?

The preface to the Ten Commandments teaches us, that because God is the Lord, and our God and Redeemer, therefore we are bound to keep all His commandments.

51. Which is the first commandment?

The first commandment is, "Thou shalt have no other Gods before me."

52. What is required in the first commandment?

The first commandment requires us to know and acknowledge God to be the only true God, and our God, and to worship and glorify Him accordingly.

53. What is forbidden in the first commandment?

The first commandment forbids the denying, or not worshiping and glorifying the true God, as God and our God; and the giving that worship and glory to any other, which is due unto Him alone.

54. What are we especially taught by these words, "before me," in the first commandment?

These words, "before me," in the first commandment, teach us, that God, who sees all things, takes notice of, and is much displeased with the sin of having any other God.

55. Which is the second commandment?

The second commandment is, "Thou shalt not make unto thee any graven image, or any likeness of any thing that is in heaven above, or that is in the earth beneath, or that is in the water under the earth. Thou shalt not bow down thyself to them, nor serve them; for I the Lord thy God am a jealous God, visiting the iniquity of the fathers upon the children, unto the third and fourth generation of them that hate me: and showing mercy unto thousands of them that love me and keep my commandments."

56. What is required in the second commandment?

The second commandment requires the receiving, observing, and keeping pure and entire, all such religious worship and ordinances, as God has appointed in His Word.

57. What is forbidden in the second commandment?

The second commandment forbids the worshiping of God by images, or any other way not appointed in His Word.

58. What are the reasons annexed to the second commandment?

The reasons annexed to the second commandment, are, God's sovereignty over us, His propriety in us, and the zeal He has for His own worship.

59. Which is the third commandment?

The third commandment is, "Thou shalt not take the name of the Lord thy God in vain: for the Lord will not hold him guiltless that taketh his name in vain."

60. What is required in the third commandment?

The third commandment requires the holy and reverent use of God's names, titles, attributes, ordinances, words, and works.

61. What is forbidden in the third commandment?

The third commandment forbids all profaning and abusing of any thing whereby God makes Himself known.

62. What is the reason annexed to the third commandment?

The reason annexed to the third commandment is, that howsoever the breakers of this commandment may escape punishment from men, yet the Lord our God will not suffer them to escape His righteous judgment.

63. Which is the fourth commandment?

The fourth commandment is, "Remember the Sabbath day to keep it holy. Six days shalt thou labor and do all thy work; but the seventh day is the Sabbath of the Lord thy God: in it thou shalt not do any work, thou, nor thy son, nor thy daughter, thy manservant, nor thy maid servant, nor thy cattle, nor thy stranger that is within thy gates: for in six days the Lord made heaven and earth, the sea, and all that in them is, and rested the seventh day: wherefore the Lord blessed the Sabbath day and hallowed it."

64. What is required in the fourth commandment?

The fourth commandment requires the keeping holy to God such set times as He has appointed in His Word, expressly one whole day in seven to be a holy Sabbath to Himself.

65. Which day of the seven has God appointed to be the weekly Sabbath?

From the creation of the world to the resurrection of Christ, God appointed the seventh day of the week to be the weekly Sabbath; and the first day of the week ever since, to continue to the end of the world, which is the Christian Sabbath.

66. How is the Sabbath to be sanctified?

The Sabbath is to sanctified by a holy resting all that day, even from such worldly employments and recreations as are lawful on other days, and spending the time in the public and private exercises of God's worship, except so much as is to be taken up in the works of necessity and mercy.

67. What is forbidden in the fourth commandment?

The fourth commandment forbids the omission or careless performance of the duties required, and the profaning the day by idleness, or doing that which is in itself sinful, or by unnecessary thoughts, words, or works, about worldly employments or recreations.

68. What are the reasons annexed to the fourth commandment?

The reasons annexed to the fourth commandment are, God's allowing us six days of the week for our own employments, His challenging a special propriety in the seventh, His own example and His blessing the Sabbath day.

69. Which is the fifth commandment?

The fifth commandment is, "Honor thy father and thy mother, that thy days may be long upon the land which the Lord thy God giveth thee."

70. What is required in the fifth commandment?

The fifth commandment requires the preserving the honor, and performing the duties, belonging to every one in their several places and relations, as superiors, inferiors, or equals.

71. What is forbidden in the fifth commandment?

The fifth commandment forbids the neglecting of, or doing anything against the honor and duty which belongs to every one in their several places and relations.

72. What is the reason annexed to the fifth commandment?

The reason annexed to the fifth commandment is a promise of long life and prosperity (as far as it shall serve God's glory and their own good), to all such as keep this commandment.

73. Which is the sixth commandment?

The sixth commandment is, "Thou shalt not kill."

74. What is required in the sixth commandment?

The sixth commandment requires all lawful endeavors to preserve our own life and the life of others.

75. What is forbidden in the sixth commandment?

The sixth commandment forbids the taking away our own life, or the life of our neighbor unjustly, or whatsoever tends thereto.

76. Which is the seventh commandment?

The seventh commandment is, "Thou shalt not commit adultery."

77. What is required in the seventh commandment?

The seventh commandment requires the preservation of our own and our neighbor's chastity, in heart, speech, and behavior.

78 What is forbidden in the seventh commandment?

The seventh commandment forbids all unchaste thoughts, words, and actions.

79. Which is the eighth commandment?

The eighth commandment is, "Thou shalt not steal."

80. What is required in the eighth commandment?

The eighth commandment requires the lawful procuring and furthering the wealth and outward state of ourselves and others.

81. What is forbidden in the eighth commandment?

The eighth commandment forbids whatsoever does or may unjustly hinder our own or our neighbor's wealth or outward state.

82. Which is the ninth commandment?

The ninth commandment is, "Thou shalt not bear false witness against thy neighbor."

83. What is required in the ninth commandment?

The ninth commandment requires the maintaining and promoting of truth between man and man, and of our own and our neighbor's good name, especially in witness bearing.

84. What is forbidden in the ninth commandment?

The ninth commandment forbids whatsoever is prejudicial to truth, or injurious to our own, or our neighbor's good name.

85. Which is the tenth commandment?

The tenth commandment is, "Thou shalt not covet thy neighbor's house. Thou shalt not covet thy neighbor's wife, nor his man servant, nor his maid servant, nor his ox, nor his ass, nor anything that is thy neighbor's."

86. What is required in the tenth commandment?

The tenth commandment requires full contentment with our own condition, with a right and charitable frame of spirit towards our neighbor, and all that is his.

87. What is forbidden in the tenth commandment?

The tenth commandment forbids all discontentment with our own estate, envying or grieving at the good of our neighbor, and all inordinate motions and affections to anything that is his.

88. Is any man able perfectly to keep the commandments of God?

No mere man, since the fall, is able in this life, perfectly to keep the commandments of God, but daily breaks them in thought, word, and deed.

89. What then is the purpose of the law since the fall?

The purpose of the law, since, the fall, is to reveal the perfect righteousness of God, that His people may know his will for their lives and the ungodly, being convicted of their sin, may be restrained therein and brought to Christ for salvation.

90. Are all transgressions of the law equally heinous?

Some sins in themselves and by reason of several aggravations, are more heinous in the sight of God than others.

91. What does every sin deserve?

Every sin deserves God's wrath and curse, both in this life, and in that which is to come.

92. What does God require of us, that we may escape His wrath and curse, due to us for sin?

To escape the wrath and curse of God due to us for sin, God requires of us faith in Jesus Christ, repentance unto life, with the diligent use of all the outward and ordinary means whereby Christ communicates to us the benefits of redemption.

93. What is faith in Jesus Christ?

Faith in Jesus Christ is a saving grace, whereby we receive and rest upon Him alone for salvation, as He is offered to us in the Gospel.

94. What is repentance unto life?

Repentance unto life is a saving grace, whereby a sinner, out of a true sense of his sin, and apprehension of the mercy of God in Christ, does, with grief and hatred of his sin, turn from it unto God, with full purpose of, and endeavor after, new obedience.

95. What are the outward and ordinary means whereby Christ communicates to us the benefits of redemption?

The outward and ordinary means whereby Christ communicates to us the benefits of redemption are His ordinances, especially the Word, Baptism, the Lord's Supper and Prayer; all which are made effectual to the elect for salvation.

96. How is the Word made effectual to salvation?

The Spirit of God makes the reading, but especially the preaching of the Word an effectual means of convincing and converting sinners, and of building them up in holiness and comfort, through faith unto salvation.

97. How is the Word to be read and heard that it may become effectual to salvation?

That the Word may become effectual to salvation we must attend thereunto with diligence, preparation and prayer, receive it in faith and love, lay it up in our hearts and practice it in our lives.

98. How do Baptism and the Lord's Supper become effectual means of salvation?

Baptism and the Lord's Supper become effectual means of salvation, not from any virtue in them or in him that administers them, but only by the blessing of Christ and the working of His Spirit in them that by faith receive them.

99. Wherein do Baptism and the Lord's Supper differ from the other ordinances of God?

Baptism and the Lord's Supper differ from the other ordinances of God in that they were specially instituted by Christ to represent and apply to believers the benefits of the new covenant by visible and outward signs.

100. What is Baptism?

Baptism is an holy ordinance, wherein the washing with water in the name of the Father, the Son and the Holy Spirit, signifies our ingrafting into Christ and partaking of the benefits of the covenant of grace, and our engagement to be the Lord's.

101. To whom is Baptism to be administered?

Baptism is to be administered to all those who actually profess repentance towards God, faith in, and obedience to our Lord Jesus Christ; and to none other.

102. Are the infants of such as are professing believers to be baptized?

The infants of such as are professing believers are not to be baptized; because there is neither command nor example in the Holy Scriptures, or certain consequence from them, to baptize such.

103. How is Baptism rightly administered?

Baptism is rightly administered by immersion, or dipping the whole body of the person in water, in the name of the Father, and of the Son, and of the Holy Spirit.

104. What is the duty of those who are rightly baptized?

It is the duty of those who are rightly baptized to give up (join) themselves to some visible and orderly church of Jesus Christ, that they may walk in all the commandments and ordinances of the Lord blameless.

105. What is the visible church?

The visible church is the organized society of professing believers, in all ages and places, wherein the Gospel is truly preached and the ordinances of Baptism and the Lord's Supper rightly administered.

106. What is the invisible church?

The invisible church is the whole number of the elect, that have been, are, or shall be gathered into one under Christ the head.

107. What is the Lord's Supper?

The Lord's Supper is a holy ordinance, wherein, by giving and receiving bread and wine, according to Christ's appointment, His death is showed forth, and the worthy receivers are, not after a corporeal and carnal manner, but by faith, made partakers of His body and blood, with all His benefits, to their spiritual nourishment, and growth in grace.

108. What is required to the worthy receiving of the Lord's Supper?

It is required of them that would worthily (that is, suitably) partake of the Lord's Supper, that they examine themselves, of their knowledge to discern the Lord's body; of their faith to feed upon Him; of their repentance, love, and new obedience: lest, coming unworthily, they eat and drink judgment to themselves.

109. What is Prayer?

Prayer is an offering up of our desires to God, for things agreeable to His will, in the name of Christ, with confession of our sins and thankful acknowledgment of His mercies.

110. What rule has God given for our direction in prayer?

The whole Word of God is of use to direct us in prayer, but the special rule of direction is that prayer, which Christ taught His disciples, commonly called the Lord's Prayer.

111. What does the preface of the Lord's Prayer teach us?

The preface of the Lord's Prayer, which is, "Our Father, which art in heaven," teaches us to draw near to God, with all holy reverence and confidence, as children to a father, able and ready to help us, and that we should pray with and for others.

112. What do we pray for in the first petition?

In the first petition, which is "Hallowed be thy name," we pray that God would enable us and others to glorify Him in all that whereby He makes Himself known, and that He would dispose all things to His own glory.

113. What do we pray for in the second petition?

In the second petition, which is "Thy kingdom come," we pray that Satan's kingdom may be destroyed, and that the kingdom of grace may be advanced; ourselves and others brought into it, and kept in it, and that the kingdom of glory may be hastened.

114. What do we pray for in the third petition?

In the third petition, which is, "Thy will be done in earth as it is in heaven," we pray that God by His grace, would make us able and willing to know, obey, and submit to His will in all things, as the angels do in heaven.

115. What do we pray for in the fourth petition?

In the fourth petition, which is, "Give us this day our daily bread," we pray that of God's free gift, we may receive a competent portion of the good things of this life and enjoy His blessing with them.

116. What do we pray for in the fifth petition?

In the fifth petition, which is, "And forgive us our debts, as we forgive our debtors," we pray that God, for Christ's sake, would freely pardon all our sins; which we are the rather encouraged to ask, because by His grace we are enabled from the heart to forgive others.

117. What do we pray for in the sixth petition?

In the sixth petition, which is, "And lead us not into temptation, but deliver us from evil," we pray that God would either keep us from being tempted to sin, or support and deliver us when we are tempted.

118. What does the conclusion of the Lord's Prayer teach us?

The conclusion of the Lord's Prayer, which is, "For thine is the kingdom, and the power, and the glory, forever, Amen," teaches us to take our encouragement in prayer from God only, and in our prayers to praise Him, ascribing kingdom, power, and glory to Him; and in testimony of our desire, and assurance to be heard, we say, AMEN.